My Brilliant
Book Buddy

Written by RITA-Award Winning, Bests-Selling Novelist

SUSAN MAY

WARREN

ISBN: 978-1-943935-03-1

Visit our Wenb site at www.mybooktherapy.com for information on more resources for writers.

To receive instruction on writing, or further help with writing projects via My Book Therapy's boutique fiction editing services, contact info@mybooktherapy.com

Susan May Warren

Susan May Warren is the Christy, RITA and Carol award-winning author of over forty-five novels with Tyndale, Barbour, Steeple Hill and Summerside Press. A prolific novelist with over 1 million books sold, Susan has written contemporary and historical romances, romantic-suspense, thrillers, rom-com and Christmas novellas. She loves to help people launch their writing careers and is the founder of www.MyBookTherapy.com and www.LearnHowtoWriteaNovel.com, a writing website that helps authors get published and stay published. She's also the author of the popular writing method, *The Story Equation.* Find excerpts and reviews of her novels at www.susanmaywarren.com

A Note from your Therapist

If you've plotted your book with How to Write a Brilliant Novel, then you have all the elements of a solid plot. And, if you've read through **Advanced Brilliant Writing**, then you have amazing moments in your book, like the one where your villain becomes Unbeatable. Or the scene where one of your Secondary Characters does exactly what the hero was about to do in a fit of Passion. Or finally, the poignant scene where your hero does that one thing that he thought he'd never do.

Keeping track of all these scenes can be overwhelming. That's why I created a My Brilliant Book Buddy, and why I'm sharing my book buddy with you. I hope he/she/it's been a help!

Let's write Brilliant Books!
Happy Writing!

Susan May Warren

Stop by www.mybooktherapy.com for more writing tips.

How do I use My Brilliant Book Buddy?

A great book takes hours of thought in every season of the manuscript--from the discovery phase, right through to the proposal and pitch.

Important, treasured thoughts. Thoughts that wake you up in the middle of the night, thoughts that dog you on your run, and thoughts that bubble out while you're cooking dinner.

Thoughts you can't lose.

More than that, with every step of the journey, you will discover new things about your characters that are essential to build into your story. But, if you were to stop writing every time you had such marvelous thoughts, you'd never get the book done!

What you need is . . . a manuscript companion.

Or . . . how about a *Book Buddy*?

You know . . . a beautiful notebook to take with you on your journey that collects your thoughts and puts them into one accessible place. It's the notebook where you build your characters, add in all those story and plot elements that make a book a best-seller, and then keep beside you as you write – or do the dishes, or keep by your bedside—to capture those amazing, fleeting, but oh-so-essential thoughts.

Think of the *Book Buddy* as that friend you talk to (instead of yourself) as you're pondering out your story.

The friend that listens. And remembers.

And joins you in the journey.

Before you start writing, sit down with your Buddy and work through your story. He'll ask you the right questions, and help you keep your framework straight and solid. Then, keep him around to remind you how to start your chapters and continue to the end. Finally, return to his questions to help you build a solid synopsis, premise, and query letter.

Oh! And don't forget to buy your Buddy some chocolate occasionally. He likes that.

Contents

Ready to begin brainstorming your book?

Sit down with your coffee, your favorite pen, and **let's start with three Big Questions:**

What is your novel about?

Why should anyone ever pick up your novel?

What is your novel's Story Question?

Remember:

Theme: Theme is the overall idea of a book or story. A **Story Question** answers a deeper question for us all, a question of the heart or mind. It's the great "what if."

 *The Book Buddy*

Now, where does *your* story fit in the list of seven great plots? Knowing this gives you some idea of how to structure your novel.

In dancing, there are the basics—the two-step, the waltz, the tango, etc. Everything else is a variation of these. Through all the storytelling in the world, a handful of basic plots reoccur--so much so that every story can be boiled down to one of these six (with variations, of course, on setting, characters and endings). If you've already developed a plot, see where yours fits in:

1. **Overcoming the Monster** – A hero on behalf of a greater good sets out to take on and slay some evil, deadly foe. We see this in movies like *Erin Brokovich, Jaws, Star Wars, The Firm, The Pelican Brief*, even one of my favorites: *Ferris Bueller's Day Off* (He's overcoming the school principal!).

2. **Rags to Riches** – Someone faces external obstacles of society or personal opposition, and the story ends with her finding the real "riches" within herself, and in the end, getting her dreams. *Cinderella, My Fair Lady*, and *Pretty Woman* are examples of this.

3. **The Great Quest – The** story's about the journey, the friends made along the journey, and how they band together to accomplish the task, win the treasure, or the war. Examples are *Raiders of the Lost Ark, National Treasure, Saving Private Ryan* – even *The Amazing Race*.

4. **Home Again, Home Again** – These are stories about people leaving the world they know, being changed by the experience, then taking those changes home and adapting them to their world. *Wizard of Oz, Sweet Home Alabama*, etc.

5. **Beast to Beauty** – A person is forced to go into a "prison" of some kind. He is finally redeemed either by an outside liberator, or by personal enlightenment. *Snow White, The Sound of Music, The Mighty Ducks, Gladiator*
    *A **Tragedy** is a takeoff of this without the happy ending. *Macbeth* or *A Beautiful Mind* shows what happens when the hero is sucked into a spell of darkness, the power of the ego. They initially might enjoy a dreamlike success, but in the end the dream turns to nightmare, and they are destroyed.

6. **See the Light** – Stories about people who are forced to re-examine who they are, or are in the middle of a misunderstanding, and they must find a new perspective to come through it and see the light. *The Devil Wears Prada, Return to Me, Chasing Liberty*

What plot is yours?

Now, let's start brainstorming your story!

"Lindy Hop" Basic Plot Structure

Basic Plot Structure
Life – Once Upon a Time
Inciting Incident – Something out of the ordinary happens
Noble Quest – Causing the protagonist to seek something
Disappointment – But things don't go as expected
Y in the Road – Forcing the protagonist to make a difficult decision
Help! – Which has consequences
Overhaul – The result of which is a change in status
Perfect Ending – And they all lived Happily Ever After (or didn't!)

Can you identify the Lindy Hop in your plot structure? (This is a general gathering of your ideas. You'll cement them later!)

Life

Inciting Incident

Noble Quest

Disappointment

Y in the Road

Help!

Overhaul

Perfect Ending

The Book Buddy

Let's meet your characters!

Character Interview: **Protagonist One**

Time to turn your focus inward. I want you to interview your character. Sit down, have a cup of coffee in hand, lock your door, and imagine your hero or heroine in your mind.

Basic Bio:

Name:

Age:

Profession:

Exploration of Dark Moment:

Tell me about the darkest moment of your past, something that shaped you.

What kind of person are you today because of that moment?

What Lie do you believe that drives you and shapes your spiritual beliefs?

What emotional wound do you carry around? What is your greatest fear?

Who are you? How would you identify yourself? (Keep asking "Why?" until you get to their motivations and values.)

What would you die for? (Noble Cause/Purpose)

What are you good at?

When the going gets tough, what do you do?

The Book Buddy

What is the happiest moment in your past?

Now let your character off the couch and take some notes.

What is your character's greatest dream? (This is some element of your character's happiest moment.)

What Truth will set him/her free?

Considering all your information: What could be a possible Black Moment for your hero/heroine?

Lindy Hop . . . Again

Now that you understand Protagonist #1 better, build a stronger Lindy Hop (Plot) for him/her:

Protagonist:

ACT 1
Life

Inciting Incident

The Big Debate

Noble Quest

ACT 2
Meet the Girl (Subplot Story begins)

Disappointment 1

Y in the Road

Disappointment 2

Y in the Road

The Book Buddy

ACT 3

Disappointment 3

      Taste of Death

Help! – Point of No Return

Overhaul/Epiphany

      Storm the Castle

Perfect Ending!

Overview of the Spiritual Journey of Protagonist #1

Step One: Spiritual Darkness – The Lie they believe

Step Two: Confirmation of the Lie – Proof (Often the Inciting Incident!)

Step Three: The Voice of Truth

Step Four: The realization of the Lie and the testing of the Truth

Step Five: The Lie is *true*, which leads to the Black Moment

Step Six: The Aha! The Truth that sets them free

Step Seven: Fighting for the Truth

Battle

Loss

Reminder

Victory

Plot	Spiritual Journey
ACT 1	
Life/Distancing	Spiritual Darkness –The Lie they believe
Inciting Incident – Denial	Confirmation of the Lie – Proof
The Big Debate	
Noble Quest	
ACT 2	
Fun and Games	
The realization of the Lie and the testing of the Truth	
Disappointment 1/Disaster	
Y in the Road	
Disappointment 2/Destruction	
Y in the Road	
Disappointment 3/Devastation	
Taste of Death	

The Book Buddy

ACT 3

Help! – Point of No Return/Black Moment	Lie feels overwhelming
Overhaul/Epiphany	The Aha! The Truth that sets them free

Fighting for the Truth

Storm the Castle (or the Final Battle)

Be attacked by the Lie

Hold onto the Truth

Seize the Day!

Perfect Ending!/Delight

Character Interview: **Protagonist Two**

Time to turn your focus inward again. I want you to interview your character. Sit down, have a cup of coffee in hand, lock your door, and imagine your hero or heroine in your mind.

Basic Bio:

Name:

Age:

Profession:

Exploration of Dark Moment:

Tell me about the darkest moment of your past, something that shaped you.

What kind of person are you today because of that moment?

What Lie do you believe that drives you and shapes your spiritual beliefs?

The Book Buddy

What emotional wound do you carry around? What is your greatest fear?

Who are you? How would you identify yourself? (Keep asking "Why?" until you get to their motivations and values)

What would you die for? (Noble Cause/Purpose)

What are you good at?

When the going gets tough, what do you do?

What is the happiest moment in your past?

Now let your character off the couch and take some notes.

What is your character's greatest dream? (This is some element of your character's happiest moment.)

What Truth will set him/her free?

Considering all your information: What could be a possible Black Moment for your hero/heroine?

The Book Buddy

Lindy Hop . . . Again:

Now that you understand Protagonist #2 better, build a stronger Lindy Hop (Plot) for him/her:

Protagonist:

ACT 1
Life

Inciting Incident

    The Big Debate

Noble Quest

ACT 2
    Meet the Girl (Subplot Story begins)

Disappointment 1

Y in the Road

Disappointment 2

Y in the Road

ACT 3

Disappointment 3

    Taste of Death

Help! – Point of No Return

Overhaul/Epiphany

    Storm the Castle

Perfect Ending!

The Book Buddy

Overview of the Spiritual Journey of Protagonist #2

Step One: Spiritual Darkness – The Lie they believe

Step Two: Confirmation of the Lie – Proof (Often the Inciting Incident!)

Step Three: The Voice of Truth

Step Four: The realization of the Lie and the testing of the Truth

Step Five: The Lie is *true*, which leads to the Black Moment

Step Six: The Aha! The Truth that sets them free

Step Seven: Fighting for the Truth

Battle

Loss

Reminder

Victory

Plot	Spiritual Journey
ACT 1	
Life/Distancing	Spiritual Darkness – The Lie they believe
Inciting Incident – Denial	Confirmation of the Lie – Proof
The Big Debate	
Noble Quest	
ACT 2	
Fun and Games	
The realization of the Lie and the testing of the Truth	
Disappointment 1/Disaster	
Y in the Road	
Disappointment 2/Destruction	
Y in the Road	
Disappointment 3/Devastation	
Taste of Death	

The Book Buddy

ACT 3

Help! – Point of No Return/Black Moment	Lie feels overwhelming
Overhaul/Epiphany	The Aha! The Truth that sets them free

Fighting for the Truth

Storm the Castle (or the Final Battle)

Be attacked by the Lie

Hold onto the Truth

Seize the Day!

Perfect Ending!/Delight

Add a *Subplot, or Layer*

A Story Layer adds depth to the plot and enhances the character struggle—and eventually his/her Epiphany. **A Story Layer deepens the *theme* of the story.**

A Subplot, however, is its own distinct story. It has an Inciting Incident, obstacles, a Black Moment, and lessons learned (and hopefully a Happily Ever After). A Subplot can mirror the main plot, and even intersect with it, but it has its own main characters, its own arc, and if pulled out of the story, could stand alone as a mini-story.

Build a Layer:

Layers are easily built into a story. Just remember these two rules:

1. **Simplicity**
   The key to a great layer is focus. You don't want to make the message complicated but, rather, deepen it.
   Define your theme. Forgiveness? Hope? Starting over?

   Now, ***what do you want to say about your theme?*** e.g. If your theme is forgiveness, do you want to say that you must forgive yourself before you can love another? That a second chance shouldn't be wasted? That hope is about looking past your present circumstances to the God who loves you?

   Finally ask: ***Is there a character in the cast who can speak into the life of the character about the —theme—eitherverbally, or through actions, or even through similar circumstances?*** (Often, we call these people Truth-tellers.)

2. Relevance

A Story Layer has to be something that relates to the main story theme.

Does it contain just an element of the entire theme? What element of the theme will you work in?

Does it speak to more than one of the characters? Whose lives does this theme touch?

Does it build on the main theme? How will you use it to deepen the main theme?

Build a Subplot

A great Subplot mirrors the theme of the main plot. It can either enhance the plot—e.g., show what could happen if one choice is made or put it in relief—or show what will happen if that choice *isn't* made. The Subplot can be a testing ground for "what if."

What lesson will the characters in my main plot learn? Is there a smaller lesson, or a piece of that lesson I can illuminate through the Subplot?

Then look at your peripheral plotting web and ask: Who is the best person to illustrate that story, either through a bad choice or a good choice?

Remember, also, a Subplot has to have all the elements of a story: Inciting incident, conflict, Black Moment, Epiphany, and a climatic ending.

A good Subplot starts after the main plot is established. Usually, I begin the Subplot after I've introduced the main characters and their conflict, often about three chapters in. Then, to keep it flowing, I usually put in one Subplot scene *or* **Point of view (POV) per every four to five main POVs. That way I keep the Subplot flowing without overwhelming the main plot. Finally, I tie up the Subplot at least three chapters before the main story ends.**

Give your Subplot Characters a Voice

A Secondary Character deepens the theme by giving the main characters a Voice of Reason or Passion.

Ask: What is my theme?

Then ask: What would the Voice of Reason do with my theme?
Look around your cast of characters. Is there anyone who can act as the Voice of Reason? Someone who reacted with reason to the situation?

What would the Voice of Passion do with my theme? Is there a character who could act as the Voice of Passion? Perhaps in a moment of fear or a moment of darkness? Maybe a friend of the hero who makes a poor decision? Or a villain who takes the theme the other way?

Which Voice do you want your Subplot or Layer characters to speak: a Voice of Passion or a Voice of Reason?

The Book Buddy

Building the Subplot or Layer Character

Creating a Subplot for your book is much like creating a main plot—you must figure out your character, and their fear and dreams and goals. However, you only have to stick to the main elements. Don't worry about the emotional journey, or even the unlayering. Keep it simple. Focus on illuminating the main theme of the plot.

Basic Bio:

Name:

Age:

Profession:

Mini-exploration of Dark Moment:

Tell me about the darkest moment of your past, something that shaped you.

What kind of person are you today because of that?

What emotional wound do you carry around? What is your greatest fear? Your Lie?

How do you feel about the theme of the story? (Example: The theme is forgiveness: Have you forgiven others? Do you need forgiveness?)

When the going gets tough, what do you do?

Now let your character off the couch and take some notes.

What is your character's greatest dream? (This is some element of your character's happiest moment)

What Truth will set him/her free?

If you are creating a story Subplot, plot out the mini-story arc:

- Inciting Incident

- Obstacle/Conflict

- Black Moment

- Epiphany (What lesson is learned?)

- Happy ending/Application by the POV characters (Main plot)

The Book Buddy

If you are creating a Layer, list two or three key scenes when your character can teach your hero/heroine a Truth about the theme. (Your character could exhibit a bad behavior or blatantly lie to the hero, which the hero later recognizes is a lie—thus leading him to the Truth. Or have your character provide your hero with a piece of the Truth he uses to build his Epiphany layer.)

Layer Scene One:

Layer Scene Two:

Layer Scene Three:

Creating the *Villain*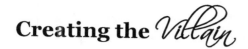

Four Components to a great Villain:

Believability. We, as the reader (and the hero) have to believe that the villain is truly *villainous*. We have to believe in our hearts that what he threatens will occur.

Believing a villain is not about looking at the villain and measuring him up. *It's about the damage he/she/it leaves behind. Think:* **Results.** A villain isn't a villain based on what he says about himself . . . but based on what he *does*.

If you want to create believability for your villain, make him/her/it do something villainous in the beginning to drive that belief home. Show him in action, or show us his handiwork.

What scene can you insert at the beginning of your book to prove to the reader that your villain's threat is believable?

The villain is one who makes it ***personal.*** Even if it's a global villain, like a nuclear war, it has to touch the life of the hero or heroine in a *personal way*. The personal connection must also be ***justified.*** It must make sense that the villain would come after the hero/heroine.

How is the threat *personal* and *justified?*

Unbeatable. A great villain, whether it be something inside us, an external force, or a green witch chasing us down a yellow road, has to be seemingly Unbeatable. The villain must be bigger than the hero. Stronger than him. Able to out-think him—even lay in wait to ambush him. **In other words, the villain must have powers *equal to* or *greater than* the hero.**

What could defeat the hero and how?

Your villain's threat is Believable, Personal, and Unbeatable. Now the key to a great villain is that it must understand the hero or heroine's greatest **tangible fear**.

How can the villain hurt the hero or heroine the most? How can he cause the hero's or heroine's greatest fear to come about?

Add in the Villainous Scenes:

One scene where the threat is Believable (Often at the beginning of the book)

One moment where the threat is Personal and Justified (Can be combined with the above scene)

One moment where the villain seems Unbeatable (Often near the Black Moment)

One moment where the villain makes the fears tangible by threatening that which is closest to your hero's heart.

The Book Buddy

The One Key Scene Every Book Should Have!

✓ What is the one thing that your character would never do?

✓ What would make him do it?

✓ What can your character sacrifice in the "One Thing" moment?

✓ Can you see the scene? Brainstorm it out.

Managing the *Muddle* (Middle!)

Now that you've figured out the "Bookends"—the beginning and end of your story—let's go back and concentrate on the middle.

You've plotted a few Disappointments (Ds) on the Journey. Now, let's make them matter!

Before we can get into the flow of the change, remember the equation of the "MUDDLE" scenes:

Push-Pull + Sympathetic Character + Stakes + Goals + Obstacle + Fear of Failure = Ds (From our character building and plotting roadmap)

For each scene in the emotional journey, confirm that you have the following:

Find the Push-Pull (Motivation): What does POV want? What does she want at this moment? Emotionally? Physically? Answering these questions helps you build the conflict.

> **Why? (do they want this?)**
> **What is the Push-Pull?** (Every scene has to have an emotional or physical Push-Pull, or combination thereof. It's the Emotional *Push* away from something, and the *Pull* toward the Happily Ever After.)

Discover what is at Stake: What will happen if they *don't* meet their goal? What fear hovers over the scene?

Create Obstacles! (Obstacles can be People or Situations—weather, or machines, or even government—but at the end, they lead to the biggest issue, and that is a person's own emotions/values.)

Increase their Fear of Failure: You've found what your character values and also, why they fear failure. It's that fear of failure—that fear of losing their values, and ultimately, themselves—that keeps the tension high.

Keeping in mind the "Muddle" equation, now you will put your character on a journey toward the Epiphany and emotional change.

Emotional Change Chart:

Act 1	Act 2	Act 3
Glimpse of Hope Invitation to change Need to change	Attempt and Failure Cost Consideration Rewards Desire Attempt and Mini-Victory Training for Battle	Black Moment Epiphany New Man (& Testing) Happily Ever After

Step One: Make sure your "Bookends" are in place

Act 1 Overview

Glimpse of Hope: Does your character see, do, or value something that indicates their need?

Here are some ideas for giving your reader that Glimpse of Hope:

1. Have your hero fail at doing something. Then have him—or someone else—comment that if only he had done or believed a certain way he might have accomplished his task. To which the hero says, "Well, that will never happen."

2. Have your hero, or just your reader, see something that the hero longs for—a happy family, a good job, a hero's welcome. Something that we can measure his later success by. I call it the glimpse of the **Happily Ever After.**

3. Have your hero hear of a story/legend/action that he wishes he could do.

Invitation to Change: The Invitation to Change is that moment when the character—very, very early on—is given the opportunity to do something different. To believe something, or value something, or try something that might change their lives. Often they turn it down, and it's that regret that drives them to have the opportunity again.

✓ Within the first three chapters, have you given your character an opportunity to believe or do something that they turn away from?

✓ Think ahead: How can you recast this choice into another moment later in the book?

Need to Change: The Need to Change is embodied in an early event or situation that should be strong and terrible enough to convince your character to grab the opportunity to change the next time it might rear its head. And, it must be a sufficient enough threat that it will force him to confront his demons and fears or beliefs—all those obstacles that will stand in the way to change.

✓ What situation, threat, loss, reward or fear would be strong enough to make your character want to change?

✓ How can you raise that need so that it looms over your character and he can't escape it?

If you were to put this into the Book Therapy Plotting Roadmap, you would plot the emotional journey alongside the Plot:

Home World/Glimpse of Hope

Inciting Incident/Invitation to Change

The Big Debate/Regret of the Missed Opportunity

Need to Change (Results in The Noble Quest)

The Book Buddy

Plot	Emotional Journey
ACT 1	
Life/Distancing	Glimpse of Hope
Inciting Incident	Invitation to Change
The Big Debate/Regret of Missed Opportunity	
Need to Change/Noble Quest	

Act 2:

Disappointment 1: Attempt (and Failure)
               Cost Consideration
               Rewards
               Desire
               Attempt and Mini-Victory
Disappointment 2: Training for Battle

Character Change: Attempt and Failure

The next stage in the journey is the hero's attempt to go after the prize, to rescue the fair maiden, or stand up to the bully, or face his fears. His attempts not only fail, but sometimes make everything worse!

✓ What attempts could your character do to change? How can you make him fail?

✓ Now make that failure worse by creating a new problem.

(This is your first Disappointment!)

Character Change: Cost Consideration

Anything worth fighting for is going to cost something. Right after he fails the first attempt, he'll have to regroup, and take a good look at his weaknesses and vacancies, and realize the Truth: If he wants victory, he can't stay the way he is.

Book Therapist Question

- ✓ What does your character have to lose if he tries again, or continues on the quest?

- ✓ Have you created enough of a motivation to sacrifice his dream despite the pain? (ie, losing something *greater*?)

Character Change: Rewards

Your character has to see past the **Costs** to the **Rewards**. And, he has to believe that it's possible. Or at least, that it could be. Seeing the Costs and the Rewards will make him look inside, to ask *why* that Reward is worth fighting for.

Later, he'll discover what it is inside him that stands in the way. But for now he has to believe that his attempt and cost is worth the battle.

So, how do you give them a Reward? Here are some ideas:

Give your character a hero. Someone who has been the course, and fought the good fight, who knows the Reward.

Give them a glimpse of the darkness. Up the ante by adding into the mix the "what if we do nothing" question. Give them a glimpse of what could happen if they *don't* fight the good fight.

Give them a cause. Do something to make them realize that if they give up, they'll lose what they love.

- ✓ Have you given your character a glimpse of the Reward that change creates, and victory?

Giving him a hero?

Showing him the alternative?

Giving him another cause to fight for?

Character Change: Creating Desire

What do you really want? When you put the cost against the Reward, and stir it together, you discover the crux of the hero's journey . . . their true desire.

- ✓ What is your character's happiest memory?

- ✓ What about that memory would he like to recreate or hold on to?

- ✓ How can you turn that memory into his greatest desire?

- ✓ How does that motivate him to pick himself back up and dive back into the fight?

The Book Buddy

Attempt and Mini-Victory

Once is not enough! Now let him win. Enough for your character to feel like they've accomplished something.

Note: the Attempt and Mini-Victory happens early in the Second Act—early enough to leave room for what is called **Training for Battle.**

✓ Have you given your character a second attempt, and a taste of victory?

Character Change: Training for Battle

Or, what I call the fun and games. Your character isn't going to literally "train for battle," but rather, be put through a number of tests. Interpersonal challenges. Physical foibles. Through which, we'll see him have to look inside and make changes.

This is the guts of the book. And the part of the story that is most easily mis-plotted. This is how you **Manage your Muddle:**

1. Every obstacle your character faces must make the journey more difficult, causing him to dig deeper and find a character trait he didn't have before.
2. He will get "better" at the skills he is developing.
3. Each time he gets better, he becomes more the person he hopes to be, a bigger Glimpse of Hope. So, give him a glimpse of something he longs for.

Training for Battle is a great way to build in micro-tension in the middle. Will your character achieve his mini-goals? And, it all feeds to the great "battle" at the end.

One key: Give your character spiritual, emotional, and physical disasters. You can separate these out into different micro-disasters, or you can create one disaster and have it affect them on three levels:

✓ Going into each scene during this section, ask yourself:

   o What losses can my character have?

   o What victories?

   o What does my character learn in this scene that makes him/her a stronger/better person?

✓ How do you give your character another Glimpse of Hope, this time in himself?

(This is where you will find your second, third, fourth, etc. Disappointments).

Act 2 culminates with a Devastating event that leads to Act 3 and the Black Moment.

The Book Buddy

ACT 2	
Attempt	Failure
Disappointment	What do they learn?
Cost Consideration	Rewards
Desire	

Attempt and Mini-Victory

Training for Battle
Disaster:

Micro-Disaster - emotional	What do they learn?
Micro-Disaster - physical	What do they learn?
Micro-Disaster - spiritual	What do they learn?

Devastation

Act 3 (You have already built these components!)

The Black Moment

Black Moment. It's when life feels overwhelming. It's when your character's worst fears come true. It's when the lie feels true and things can't get any worse.

The Epiphany

The **Epiphany** is the recognition of some faulty belief or wrong action that has handicapped your character and then the realization of what I call the **Truth that sets them Free.**

✓ What can they look past and recognize?

✓ What can they look forward and realize? (What Truth sets them free?)

Character Change: He's a New Man!

In some way, we need to see that our character is a **New Man**. The best way to do this is to test him by making him fight for the Truth through: **Final Battle, Loss, Reminder, Victory.**

- Final Battle:
- Loss:
- Reminder:
- Victory:

The **Final Battle** is the last challenge they must face. Storming the castle, running after the girl, facing the villain—whatever they've been preparing for the entire book.

What is your hero's Final Battle?

The **Loss** represents an obstacle in the way, some derailment of their quest—from a defeat to a death—but some element of loss. It can also occur when the Lie attacks him a final time.

How does the Lie attack?

The **Reminder** is just that: a reminder of his Epiphany, the Truth that has set him free, reminding him that he is a New Man. Your character grasps this Epiphany, this Truth, and holds on for dear life, making it a part of him.

What is the reminder of the Truth?

Finally, the **Victory** is the New Man changed, the accomplishment of his goals, and the happy ending.

What does he/she achieve that is a part of their greatest dreams?

Happily Ever After

The New home world of your character.
How do you show a new world for your character?

 *The Book Buddy*

ACT 3	

Devastation/Black Moment

Epiphany/Aha! Truth that sets them free!

New Man/Final Battle

Loss/Lie

Reminder/Hold onto the Truth

Victory!

Happily Ever After

Creating the *Inciting Incident*:

The Inciting Incident delivery demands an exquisite balance of **delicacy** and **resonance.**

Delicacy and Resonance?

Delicacy in the Inciting Incident doesn't mean a light touch. It means treading lightly through Backstory, digging up only that which is most pertinent.

Resonance, of course, is *meaning*. We want to know how this event fits into the Story Question, as well as the past. We also want to understand what the next step is for the character.

The BIG BANG: Believability, Action, Need, Genre

Believability – Do you need to build sympathy for your character before the Inciting Incident will have an impact on the reader? How much Backstory do you need to create believability?

Action – Generally, the higher the action, the closer it should be to the beginning of the book.

Need – Your character starts out with a need. What can you build into that Inciting Incident that reveals that need?

Genre – Certain genres demand different Inciting Incidents.

Developing the Big Bang!

✓ What **Believable** incident could occur in your hero's/heroine's home world? How much sympathy do you need to build for your character to have the reader care that he/she's facing this incident?

✓ What **Actions** could he/she take, or have happen to him/her?

✓ What is (are) your character's primary **Needs**?

✓ What **Genre** are you writing? Look at your pile of genre books and read the first chapter, or at least the first page, of three of them. What happens? What ideas does this churn up for your hero/heroine?

✓ Finally, what Backstory elements do you need to include in order to give the Inciting Incident **Delicacy and Resonance**?

The Book Buddy

Okay, so you know *where* to place the Inciting Incident. But now the question is: *How?*

The Six Elements to an Inciting Incident!

Sympathy - Ask yourself, what situation can I put my hero/heroine in that would make my audience feel for him/her? What collective experience or feeling can I touch on that makes him/her instantly identifiable and creates reader sympathy?

Stakes - Why should the reader care about this situation, this story? Hint at this in the first scene.

Motivation - What about this situation motivates your hero/heroine to move to the next step in the journey?

Desires - What is at stake that our hero/heroine cares about, longs for, dreams of?

Fears - What is your hero/heroine deeply afraid of?

Action words - Use vivid descriptions and active, strong verbs. Pick the right words to convey mood, and give the scene texture.

Inciting Incident *Checklist:*

✓ What sympathetic situation is your character in?

✓ What's at stake in this scene? In the book?

✓ What are your hero's/heroine's values? What motivations do they lead to?

✓ What are your hero's/heroine's desires or fears? How can you use them to build tension in the scene?

✓ Now, go through your scene and replace all the passive verbs with strong action verbs.

Let's do it again! (For Protagonist #2)

Big Bang:

- ✓ What **Believable** incident could occur in your hero's/heroine's home world? How much sympathy do you need to build for your character to have the reader care that he's/she's facing this incident?

- ✓ What **Actions** could he/she take, or have happen to him/her?

- ✓ What is (are) your character's primary **Needs**?

- ✓ What **Genre** are you writing? Look at your pile of genre books and read the first chapter, or at least the first page, of three of them. What happens? What ideas does this churn up for your hero/heroine?

- ✓ Finally, what Backstory elements do you need to include in order to give the Inciting Incident **Delicacy and Resonance**?

The Book Buddy

The Six Elements to an Inciting Incident!

Sympathy - Ask yourself, what situation can I put my hero/heroine in that would make my audience feel for him/her? What collective experience or feeling can I touch on that makes him/her instantly identifiable and creates reader sympathy?

Stakes - Why should the reader care about this situation, this story? Hint at this in the first scene.

Motivation - What about this situation motivates your hero/heroine to move to the next step in the journey?

Desires - What is at stake that your hero/heroine cares about, longs for, dreams of?

Fears - What is your hero/heroine deeply afraid of?

Action words - Use vivid descriptions and active, strong verbs. Pick the right words to convey mood, and give the scene texture.

Inciting Incident *Checklist:*

✓ What sympathetic situation is your character in?

✓ What's at stake in this scene? In the book?

✓ What are your hero's/heroine's values, and what motivations do they lead to?

✓ What are your hero's/heroine's desires or fears? How can you use them to build tension in the scene?

✓ Now, go through your scene and replace all the passive verbs with strong action verbs.

(If you want, this would be a *great* time to flesh out your synopsis. You have all the ingredients of your story. Why not?)

To help you along, here are:

Story Synopsis Pieces

Life – Five Ws – The Set-up
                     Identity/Competence/Goal/Wound/Lie/GF/GD
      Inciting Incident –
         What happens that ignites the story and gives the character a choice
         The Big Debate – What should they do?
      Noble Quest—What your character's goal is—and what stands in their way
         (+ Promise of the theme: Spiritual Takeaway)

Disappointment 1 + Y in the Road
      (Goal/Motivation/Conflict or GMC for each) (Turning Point 1)
Disappointment 2 + Y in the Road (Turning Point 2)
Disappointment 3 + Taste of Death (Turning Point 3)

Point of No Return/Black Moment
      Overhaul/Epiphany – The Truth that sets them free
Storm the Castle – the final scene (Climax)
Perfect Ending – thematic statement – wrap up

(Note: I often skip the Subplot or layer when writing the synopsis as it complicates the synopsis.

Or, I'll write a separate synopsis, if it is a subplot.)

Hey wait! We're not done yet!

The Book Buddy

Or you could . . .

Write your first chapter!

Let's start with an overview of the elements:

POV:

Structure:
     Action Objectives:

     Goal:

     Conflict:

     Disaster:

Texture:
     Smells -

     Sounds - (including voices)

     Sights -

     Touch -

     Taste -

     Details you could use for a metaphor:

     Character Emotional Hues:

Getting Started:

The Facts:

Who :

What

Where

When

Why

HOOK:

Stakes

Hero/Heroine Identification   .

Anchoring

Run (Starting with the scene already in action)

Problem/Story Question

What is your POV Character thinking *right now*? This could be your first line!

The Book Buddy

First Chapter Checklist:

These are things that you need to make sure you're communicating in the first chapter.

✓ Have you created sympathy for your character so we love them?

✓ Have you shown us your character's home life, so we know where their journey begins?

✓ Have you shown us your character's competence, and their identity?

✓ Have you given us a glimpse of your character's Greatest Dream?

✓ Have you given us a hint of your character's Greatest Fear?

✓ Have you given us a hint at your character's Spiritual Lie?

✓ Have you set the mood of the book (suspense/mystery/fantasy, women's fiction, rom-com, romance, etc).

✓ Have you delivered the Story Question that will drive us through the book?

✓ Do you have crisp, interesting dialogue?

✓ Have you honed your hook to include the Who, What, Where, When and Why of the story?

✓ Do you have sufficient Storyworld?

✓ Have you used the five senses?

✓ Have you shown us the story in active voice?

✓ Have you used specific nouns and vivid verbs to add emotion to the story?

✓ Have you ended the scene with a disaster, or something that makes the reader want to turn the page?

Now, all you have to do is *do this for every scene*!

Need Help?

> **Turn to the Appendix for:**
> Action Scene Starter/Set up Sheets
> ReAction Scene Starter/Set up Sheets
> Combo Scenes Starter/Set up Sheets

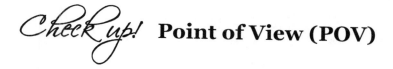 **Point of View (POV)**

Determine the POV VOICE for this book:

Take your main character and put him in a scene.

> Write the scene from the First Person POV. Reactions? Did you like this voice? Why/Why not?

> Now try it from the Third-Person POV. Reactions? Did you like this voice? Why/Why not?

Which seems stronger to you?

Are you using the right POV?

Multiple POV choice: Who else is in the scene?

- ✓ Out of the lineup of cast members, who has the most at stake in the scene?

- ✓ Who would react strongest to the situation, emotionally or physically?

- ✓ What POV has the most reader impact? Are you using the correct POV for this scene?

Check up! Dialogue

Pick a scene with dialogue to give your characters' conversation a check up.

- ✓ What do the characters in the scene each need to accomplish, and what emotions will they display?

- ✓ What do they really want to say? Have you ignored your first instinct and written their true emotions?

- ✓ What is the one tone of voice you could insert that would add impact?

- ✓ What action could they do to accentuate their words? What is the appropriate body language for their attitude and what could they be hiding?

- ✓ Have you inserted fighting words/zingers?

 **Storyworld**

- ✓ How does your POV character feel about being in the Storyworld?

- ✓ What one internal thought could he have that reveals this feeling?

- ✓ What physical response does he/she have that reveals this feeling/attitude? Think: Senses cause physical responses.

- ✓ What noun, adjective, or verb could you use that adds prejudice to his/her thoughts, speech, or actions?

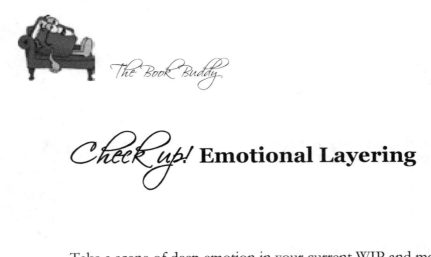

The Book Buddy

Check up! Emotional Layering

Take a scene of deep emotion in your current WIP and make it Soul-Deep.

Step one: Find the one emotion you want to convey.

Step two: What nouns, verbs, and metaphors can you build into the scene to convey the emotion of your character?

Step three: Is there another person in the scene you can use for character comparison?

Step four: What is the one action you can do to convey the character's emotional state?

Now, write the scene without naming the emotion!

64

 **Word Painting**

FOCUS: First Impression, Observations, Close Up, and Simile (or Metaphor)

First Impression is all about giving us that overview of the setting. For example, if you were walking into a conference room, you might say: *The conference room was small but comfortable.* But you could make it stronger with more specific nouns, some POV added. Example: *The owner had designed this room with an eye toward productivity, not power.*

Then, go to the **Observations** and show a few notable items. Be specific with you nouns and verbs so you lend a mood without saying outright what that mood is. Example: *No table, just four espresso-brown leather couches like his living room on the ranch, and a couple cigar chairs all in a Camelot circle in the center of the room.*

Then, do a **Close Up** of some details that really make the room stand out. Example: *His secretary had brewed a fresh pot of coffee, and a tray of bagels sat in the middle of the round coffee table.*

Finally, end with **Symbolic language**, a metaphor or simile, something that lends a feeling about the place. Example: *Through the giant picture window, he saw sailboats cutting through the Puget Sound like surrender flags against a pristine blue sky. He checked his watch even as he sat down. He hoped no one got too comfortable.*

✓ *Exercise: Find one element of static description in your scene, and FOCUS it.*

Active Description:

Create a metaphorical word pool. As you write, your words will tend toward specific verbs and nouns. Taking a step away from these, you'll find that they might fall in categories of description. Use them as an "emotional" or "metaphorical" thesaurus.

Pick Verbs that convey the *feeling* of what you are describing. If I were describing a giant crater in the earth, one made by a meteor, I might use words like "jagged," "ripped," and "bruised." But if I were describing a hole that would become my long desired swimming pool, I'd go with "scooped," or even "carved" from the earth.

✓ *Exercise: Take one active description, create a metaphorical word pool, and rewrite the description.*

Premise (Getting ready to pitch!)

Write a loose paragraph about your story—whatever comes to mind.
(Think about your character, the Black Moment, the Epiphany, and what's at stake.)

Now, step by step, pull out your Premise:

Step One: Character identity

Step Two: Goals

Step Three: Conflict

Step Four: Stakes

Step Five: Story Question

Step Six: Powerful words

Now **Recast your Premise** with the powerful words you've chosen. Write it on an index card and post it over your computer. Memorize it. The next time someone asks what your novel is about, you can tell them!

Query Letter

Let's break your query letter down into the essential pieces:

Hook

Summary

Marketability

Who/Why

Mechanics

The Book Buddy

Extras! (Appendix)

Character Building: Protagonist

Basic Bio:

Name:

Age:

Profession:

Exploration of Dark Moment:

Tell me about the darkest moment of your past, something that shaped you.

What kind of person are you today because of that moment?

What Lie do you believe that drives you and shapes your spiritual beliefs?

What emotional wound do you carry around? What is your greatest fear?

Who are you? How would you identify yourself? (Keep asking "Why?" until you get to your character's motivations and values)

What would you die for? (Noble Cause/Purpose)

What are you good at?

When the going gets tough, what do you do?

The Book Buddy

What is the happiest moment in your past?

Now let your character off the couch and take some notes.

What is your character's greatest dream? (This is some element of your character's happiest moment.)

What Truth will set him/her free?

Considering all your information: What could be a possible Black Moment for your hero/heroine?

Character Building: Protagonist

Basic Bio:

Name:

Age:

Profession:

Exploration of Dark Moment:

Tell me about the darkest moment of your past, something that shaped you.

What kind of person are you today because of that moment?

What Lie do you believe that drives you and shapes your spiritual beliefs?

What emotional wound do you carry around? What is your greatest fear?

Who are you? How would you identify yourself? (Keep asking "Why?" until you get to your character's motivations and values.)

What would you die for? (Noble Cause/Purpose)

What are you good at?

When the going gets tough, what do you do?

What is the happiest moment in your past?

Now let your character off the couch and take some notes.

What is your character's greatest dream? (This is some element of your character's happiest moment.)

What Truth will set him/her free?

Considering all your information: What could be a possible Black Moment for your hero/heroine?

Building the Subplot or Layer Character

Basic Bio:

Name:

Age:

Profession:

Mini-exploration of Dark Moment:

Tell me about the darkest moment of your past, something that shaped you.

What kind of person are you today because of that?

What emotional wound do you carry around? What is your greatest fear? Your Lie?

How do you feel about the theme of the story? (Example: The theme is forgiveness. Have you forgiven others? Do you need forgiveness?)

When the going gets tough, what do you do?

Now let your character off the couch and take some notes.

What is your character's greatest dream? (This is some element of your character's happiest moment.)

If you are creating a story Subplot, plot out the min-story arc:

- Inciting Incident

- Obstacle/Conflict

- Black Moment

- Epiphany (What is the lesson learned?)

- Happy ending/Application by the POV characters (Main plot)

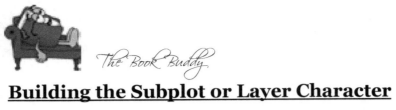

The Book Buddy

Building the Subplot or Layer Character

Basic Bio:

Name:

Age:

Profession:

Mini-exploration of Dark Moment:

Tell me about the darkest moment of your past, something that shaped you.

What kind of person are you today because of that?

What emotional wound do you carry around? What is your greatest fear? Your Lie?

How do you feel about the theme of the story? (Example: The theme is forgiveness. Have you forgiven? Do you need forgiveness?)

When the going gets tough, what do you do?

Now let your character off the couch and take some notes.

What is your character's greatest dream? (This is some element of your character's happiest moment.)

What Truth will set him/her free?

If you are creating a story Subplot, plot out the mini-story arc:

- Inciting Incident

- Obstacle/Conflict

- Black Moment

- Epiphany (What lesson is learned?)

- Happy ending/Application by the POV characters (Main plot)

<u>Overview of Spiritual Journey</u>

Name:

Step One: Spiritual Darkness— The Lie they believe

Step Two: Confirmation of the Lie – Proof (Often the Inciting Incident!)

Step Three: The Voice of Truth

Step Four: The realization of the Lie and the testing of the Truth

Step Five: The Lie is *true*, which leads to Black Moment

Step Six: The Aha! The Truth that sets them free

Battle

Loss

Reminder

Victory

The Book Buddy

Overview of the Spiritual Journey

Name:

Step One: Spiritual Darkness— The Lie they believe

Step Two: Confirmation of the Lie – Proof (Often the Inciting Incident!)

Step Three: The Voice of Truth

Step Four: The realization of the Lie and the testing of the Truth

Step Five: The Lie is *true*, which leads to Black Moment

Step Six: The Aha! The Truth that sets them free

Step Seven: Fighting for the Truth

   Battle

   Loss

   Reminder

   Victory

The Book Buddy

Plot	Emotional Journey
ACT 1	
Life/Distancing	Glimpse of Hope
Inciting Incident	Invitation to Change
The Big Debate/Regret of Missed Opportunity	
Need to Change/Noble Quest	

ACT 2

Attempt

Failure

Disappointment

What do they learn?

Cost Consideration

Rewards

Desire

The Book Buddy

ACT 3	

Devastation/Black Moment

Epiphany/Aha! Truth that sets them free!

New Man/Final Battle

Loss/Lie

Reminder/Hold onto the Truth

Victory!

Happily Ever After

The Book Buddy

Reminder/Hold onto the Truth

Victory!

Happily Ever After

Emotional Journey Chart:

Plot	Emotional Journey
ACT 1	
Life/Distancing	Glimpse of Hope
Inciting Incident	Invitation to Change
The Big Debate/Regret of Missed Opportunity	
Need to Change/Noble Quest	

87

The Book Buddy

ACT 2	
Attempt	Failure
Disappointment	What do they learn?
Cost Consideration	Rewards
Desire	

Attempt and Mini-Victory

Training for Battle
Disaster:

Micro-Disaster - emotional	What do they learn?
Micro-Disaster - physical	What do they learn?
Micro-Disaster - spiritual	What do they learn?

Devastation

The Book Buddy

ACT 3	
Devastation/Black Moment	
Epiphany/Aha! Truth that sets them free!	
New Man/Final Battle	
Loss/Lie	

Reminder/Hold onto the Truth

Victory!

Happily Ever After

The Book Buddy

Action Scene:

POV:

Structure:
    Action Objectives:

    Goal:

    Conflict:

    Disaster:

Texture:
    Smells -

    Sounds (including voices!) -

    Sights -

    Touch -

    Taste -

    Details you could use for a metaphor:

    Character Emotional Hues:

<u>Getting Started:</u>

The Facts:

Who:

What:

When:

Where:

Why:

HOOK:

Stakes

Hero/Heroine Identification

Anchoring

Run (Starting with the scene already in action)

Problem/Story Question

What is your POV Character thinking *right now*? This could be your first line!

The Book Buddy

ReAction Scene:

POV:

Structure:

    Action Objectives:

    Response:

    Dilemma:

    Decision:

Texture:

    Smells -

    Sounds (including voices!) -

    Sights -

    Touch -

    Taste -

    Details you could use for a metaphor:

    Character Emotional Hues:

Getting Started:

The Facts:

Who:

What:

When:

Where:

Why:

HOOK:

Stakes

Hero/Heroine Identification

Anchoring

Run (Starting with the scene already in action)

Problem/Story Question

What is your POV Character thinking *right now*? This could be your first line!

The Book Buddy

Combo ReAction/Action Scene:

POV:

Structure:

    Response:

    Dilemma:

    Decision:

Action Objectives:

    Goal:

    Conflict:

    Disaster:

Texture:

    Smells -

    Sounds (including voices) -

    Sights -

    Touch -

    Taste -

    Details you could use for a metaphor:

    Character Emotional Hues:

Getting Started:

The Facts:

Who:

What:

Where:

When:

Why:

HOOK:
Stakes

Hero/Heroine Identification

Anchoring

Run (Starting with the scene already in action)

Problem/Story Question

What is your POV Character thinking *right now*? This could be your first line!

How to Write a Brilliant Novel

The easy, step-by-step method of crafting a powerful story

What does it take to write a brilliant novel? Susan May Warren knows exactly how--and you're about to find out. She's coached hundreds of writers into publication, onto best-seller lists, and onto the awards platforms. (And she lives what she teaches. Susan is the bestselling author of over 50 novels, has won the Rita, the Christy, and the Carol awards multiple times.) Now, for the first time, she's revealing her step-by-step story crafting secrets that will show you how to discover, create, and publish the brilliant novel inside you.

Susan's techniques are proven methods that will show you:

- Exactly how bestselling novels are designed

- How to create compelling characters

- How to construct tension-filled scenes. . .that keep readers devouring pagesHow to build sizzling dialogue

- How to develop riveting plots that keep readers guessingAnd once you're finished, how to sell your novel

You CAN Write a Brilliant Novel!

"A quirky, fun, practical guide from a writer who knows what she's doing." -- James Scott Bell, bestselling author of *Write Great Fiction:Plot & Structure*.

Best-selling, award-winning novelist and writing coach
Susan May Warren

Make your plot wider and your characters deeper.

Advanced Brilliant Writing

An amazing novel has two elements – deep characterization of a sympathetic hero, and a compelling, wide, breathtaking plot. But how do you create deep characters and wide plots and then apply them to your story? It's time to learn Advanced (Brilliant!) Writing. The follow-up to How to Write a Brilliant Novel, Advanced Brilliant Writing utilizes RITA and Christy award-winning, best-selling novelist Susan May Warren's easy to apply explanations, exercises and intuitive methods to teach you advanced fiction writing techniques that will turn any novel from boring to . . . brilliant.

You'll learn:

- How to plot a profound character change journey

- An easy technique to reveal backstory to your readers

- How to weave emotion into your scene for the most impact

- How to keep tension high through the use of stakes and motivations

- A unique plotting trick to widen your plot

- Techniques on how to make your hero…heroic

- The difference between subplots and layers

- A powerful use for Secondary characters

- How the perfect Villain can help you plot your story

. . . and much more, including the scene that every book MUST have!

"If you're intending to write a best-selling novel, I can think of no better place to start than with Susan May Warren's Deep and Wide. This is a book for those who need to dig into the techniques of writing -- not just hear the happy-talk, big-picture stuff that is so often heard at conferences. If you really want to get into the nuts and bolts of writing strong fiction, then this is for you. Clear, practical advice from an award-winning novelist." *Chip MacGregor, Literary Agent, MacGregor Literary*

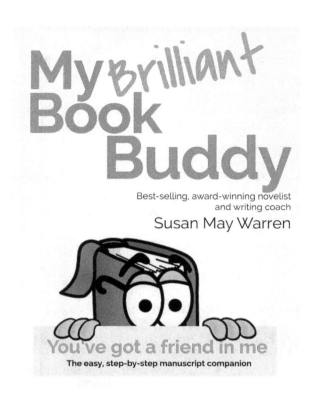

My Brilliant Book Buddy

The writing journey can be long and lonely. It's easy to get lost in the weeds of your story, not sure where you are headed . . . or why. Wouldn't it be nice to have a guide along the way? Someone to point you in the right direction, and keep you motivated.

A manuscript companion to the foundational writer's workbook How to Write a Brilliant Novel, and advanced writer's guide, Advanced Brilliant Writing, My Brilliant Book Buddy puts feet to all the steps needed to create a powerful book, guiding you through character creation, plotting the inner and outer journey, creating essential scenes, and word-painting. With step-by-step instruction, it helps you craft the perfect black moment, and pushes you on all the way to the climatic ending.

"The Book Buddy is my new best friend! It takes all of the helpful tools, charts and tips from Inside Out and Deep and Wide and puts them in one place. It's like having Susan May Warren in the room helping you craft your story! I can't recommend it highly enough! *Melissa Tagg, multi-published romance author*

How to Write a Brilliant Romance

The easy, step-by-step method of crafting a powerful romance

What does it take to write a brilliant romance? Susan May Warren knows exactly how--and you're about to find out.

Now, for the first time, she's revealing her step-by-step romance writing secrets that will show you how to craft an award-winning romance.

Secrets like:

- How do I structure my romance?

- How do I create likeable heroes and heroines?

- How should my hero and heroine meet?

- How do I make two characters fall in love?

- How do I write a sizzling kiss?

- How do I create believable conflict?

- How do I keep the tension high in the middle of my story?

- How do I put romance on every page?

- What is the breakup and why do I need it?

- Most importantly, how do I create an unique romance that touches the heart of my reader?

Find the answers to all these questions as well as a few secrets to creating award-winning romances.

With ten ingredients and step by step instructions you'll learn how to plot and write a powerful, layered romance designed to win readers. Susan May Warren has coached hundreds of writers into publication, onto best-seller lists, and onto the awards platforms. (And she lives what she teaches. Susan is the bestselling author of over 50 novels, has won the Rita, the Christy, and the Carol awards multiple times.)

Did you like this book? Thank you for reading!

I love to help authors with their craft, encouraging them and
equipping them with tools to get published and stay published. I do hope you enjoyed our "conversations" and that they
helped you as you grew your story.

If you're interested in more resources on writing craft, or even growing your career as a novelist, check out our website:
www.mybooktherapy.com. Sign up to receive the daily dose of writing craft, and check out our programs and/or events. We have something for everyone!

If this book clicked with you, I'd be ever so grateful if you'd
share that with me (susan@mybooktherapy.com) and others by way of a review on Amazon.com.

Go – write something brilliant!

CPSIA information can be obtained
at www.ICGtesting.com
Printed in the USA
LVHW061347070519
616940LV00027B/452/P